.50

# SIT, WALK, STAND

D0925451

# WATCHMAN NEE

# Sit
# Walk
# Stand

CHRISTIAN LITERATURE CRUSADE
FORT WASHINGTON          PENNSYLVANIA

First published in 1957
by Gospel Literature Service, Bombay.
Fourth and revised edition 1962
Reprinted 1963
Reprinted 1964
Reprinted 1965
Reprinted 1966
Reprinted 1967


CHRISTIAN LITERATURE CRUSADE

CANADA
1440 Mackay Street, Montreal, Quebec

GREAT BRITAIN
39 Ludgate Hill, London, E.C.4

AUSTRALIA
Eastwood, Sydney, New South Wales

NEW ZEALAND
Box 1688, Auckland, C.1

*Also in:*

Europe, South America, Caribbean Area,
Africa, India, Indonesia, Philippines,
Pakistan, Japan, Middle East,
Korea, Thailand, New Guinea


Printed in Great Britain
by Richard Clay (The Chaucer Press), Ltd., Bungay, Suffolk

# PREFACE TO THE FOURTH EDITION

Compiled from the spoken ministry of Mr Watchman Nee (Nee To-sheng) of Foochow and first published in Bombay, *Sit, Walk, Stand* continues to stir the hearts of readers with its arousing message. Although through successive editions the book has been slightly expanded, all the source material dates from a single period—the spacious days of evangelistic witness in China just prior to the Japanese war, when the author and his fellow Christians enjoyed a liberty in the service of God that is rare today. A message which expresses at once their triumphant assurance in the finished work of Christ and their humble sense of the high qualities called for in His servants has a fresh relevance for us now, when Christian work everywhere is on trial. May God give us grace not only to heed its challenge but to find ways, while there is time, of applying its lessons in our own sphere of opportunity.

London, 1962                                    Angus I. Kinnear

# INTRODUCTION

If the life of a Christian is to be pleasing to God it must be properly adjusted to Him in all things. Too often we place the emphasis in our own lives upon the application of this principle to some single detail of our behaviour or of our work for Him. Often we fail therefore to appreciate either the extent of the adjustment called for or, at times even, the point from which it should begin. But God measures everything, from start to finish, by the perfections of His Son. Scripture clearly affirms that it is God's good pleasure 'to sum up all things in Christ . . . in whom also we were made a heritage' (Eph. 1. 9–11). It is my earnest prayer that, in the discussion that follows, our eyes may be opened afresh to see that it is only by placing our entire emphasis *there* that we can hope to realise the divine purpose for us, which is that 'we should be unto the praise of his glory' (1. 12).

We shall take as a background to our thoughts the Epistle of Paul to the Ephesians.

Like so many of the apostle's letters, this Epistle falls naturally into two sections, a doctrinal and a practical. The doctrinal section (chapters 1 to 3) is concerned mainly with the great facts of the redemption which God has wrought for us in Christ. The practical section (chapters 4 to 6) then goes on to present us with the demands, in terms of Christian conduct and zeal, that God is making upon us in the light of that redemption. The two halves are closely related, but it will be seen that the emphasis in each is different.

Then, further, the second and more obviously practical

half of the letter may again conveniently be subdivided according to its subject-matter into a first long section from chapter 4. 1 to 6. 9 and a second and much shorter section from chapter 6. 10 to the end. The first part deals with our life in the midst of the world; the second with our conflict with the devil.

Thus we have, in all, three sub-divisions of the Epistle to the Ephesians, setting forth the believer's position in Christ (1. 1–3. 21), his life in the world (4. 1–6. 9), and his attitude to the enemy (6. 10–24). We may summarise these as follows:

EPHESIANS

A. Doctrinal (Chapters 1 to 3)

1. OUR POSITION IN CHRIST (1. 1–3. 21)

B. Practical (Chapters 4 to 6)

2. OUR LIFE IN THE WORLD (4. 1–6. 9)

3. OUR ATTITUDE TO THE ENEMY (6. 10–24)

Of all Paul's epistles, it is in Ephesians that we find the highest spiritual truths concerning the Christian life. The letter abounds with spiritual riches, and yet at the same time it is intensely practical. The first half of the letter reveals our life in Christ to be one of union with Him in the highest heavens. The second half shows us in very practical terms how such a heavenly life is to be lived by us down here on the earth. We do not here propose to study the letter in detail. We shall, however, touch on a few principles lying at its heart. For this purpose we shall select one key-word in each of the above three sections to express what we believe to be its governing idea.

In the first section of the letter we note the word *sit* (2. 6) which is the key to that section and the secret of a true Christian experience. God has made us to sit with Christ in the heavenly places, and every Christian must begin his spiritual life from that place of rest. In the second part we select the work *walk* (4. 1) as expressive of our life in the world, which is its subject. We are challenged there to display in our Christian walk conduct that is in keeping with our high calling. And finally, in the third part we find the key to our attitude towards the enemy contained in the one word *stand* (6. 11), expressive of our place of triumph at the end. Thus we have:

KEY WORDS IN EPHESIANS

1. Our Position in Christ—'SIT' (2. 6)
2. Our Life in the World—'WALK' (4. 1)
3. Our Attitude to the Enemy—'STAND' (6. 11)

The life of the believer always presents these three aspects—to God, to man, and to the Satanic powers. To be useful in God's hand a man must be properly adjusted in respect of all three: his position, his life, and his warfare. He falls short of God's requirements if he underestimates the importance of any one of them, for each is a sphere in which God would express 'the glory of his grace, which he freely bestowed on us in the Beloved' (1. 6).

We will take, then, these three words—'Sit', 'Walk', 'Stand'—as guides to the teaching of the Epistle, and as the text for its present message to our hearts. We shall find it most instructive to note both the order and the connection in which they come.

# I

# SIT

'*The God of our Lord Jesus Christ, . . . raised him from the dead, and made him to sit at his right hand in the heavenly places, far above all rule, and authority, and power, and dominion, and every name that is named, not only in this world, but also in that which is to come*' (*1. 17–21*).

'*And raised us up with him, and made us to sit with him in the heavenly places, in Christ Jesus: . . . for by grace have ye been saved through faith; and that not of yourselves: it is the gift of God: not of works, that no man should glory*' (*2. 6–9*).

'God . . . made him to sit . . . and made us to sit with him.' Let us first consider the implications of this word 'sit'. As we have said, it reveals the secret of a heavenly life. Christian life does not begin with walking; it begins with sitting. The Christian era began with Christ, of whom we are told that, when He had made purification of sins, He 'sat down on the right hand of the Majesty on high' (Heb. 1. 3). With equal truth we can say that the individual Christian life begins with a man 'in Christ'—that is to say, when by faith we see ourselves seated together with Him in the heavens.

Most Christians make the mistake of trying to walk in order to be able to sit, but that is a reversal of the true order. Our natural reason says, If we do not walk, how can we ever reach the goal? What can we attain without effort? How can we ever get anywhere if we do not move? But Christianity is a queer business! If at the out-

11

set we try to do anything, we get nothing; if we seek to
attain something, we miss everything. For Christianity
begins not with a big DO, but with a big DONE. Thus
Ephesians opens with the statement that God *has* 'blessed
us with every spiritual blessing in the heavenly places in
Christ' (1. 3) and we are invited at the very outset to sit
down and enjoy what God has done for us; not to set out
to try and attain it for ourselves.

Walking implies effort, whereas God says that we are
saved, not by works, but 'by grace ... through faith'
(2. 8). We constantly speak of being 'saved through
faith', but what do we mean by it? We mean this, that we
are saved by reposing in the Lord Jesus. We did nothing
whatever to save ourselves; we simply laid upon Him the
burden of our sin-sick souls. We began our Christian life
by depending not upon our own doing but upon what He
had done. Until a man does this he is no Christian; for
to say: 'I can do nothing to save myself; but by His grace
God *has done* everything for me in Christ', is to take the
first step in the life of faith. The Christian life from start
to finish is based upon this principle of utter dependence
upon the Lord Jesus. There is no limit to the grace God
is willing to bestow upon us. He will give us everything,
but we can receive none of it except as we rest in Him.
'Sitting' is an attitude of rest. Something has been
finished, work stops, and we sit. It is paradoxical, but
true, that we only advance in the Christian life as we learn
first of all to sit down.

What does it really mean to sit down? When we walk
or stand we bear on our legs all the weight of our own
body, but when we sit down our entire weight rest upon
the chair or couch on which we sit. We grow weary when
we walk or stand, but we feel rested when we have sat
down for a while. In walking or standing we expend a

great deal of energy, but when we are seated we relax at
once, because the strain no longer falls upon our muscles
and nerves but upon something outside of ourselves. So
also in the spiritual realm, to sit down is simply to rest our
whole weight—our load, ourselves, our future, everything—upon the Lord. We let Him bear the responsibility and cease to carry it ourselves.

This was God's principle from the beginning. In the
creation God worked from the first to the sixth day and
rested on the seventh. We may truthfully say that for
those first six days He was very busy. Then, the task He
had set Himself completed, He ceased to work. The
seventh day became the sabbath of God; it was God's rest.

But what of Adam? Where did he stand in relation to
that rest of God? Adam, we are told, was created on the
sixth day. Clearly, then, he had no part in those first six
days of work, for he came into being only at their end.
God's seventh day was, in fact, Adam's first. Whereas
God worked six days and then enjoyed His sabbath rest,
Adam began his life with the sabbath; for God works
before He rests, while man must first enter into God's
rest, and then alone can he work. Moreover it was because God's work of creation was truly complete that
Adam's life could begin with rest. And here is the Gospel: that God has gone one stage further and has completed also the work of redemption, and that we need do
nothing whatever to merit it, but can enter by faith
directly into the values of His finished work.

Of course we know that between these two historic
facts, between God's rest in creation and God's rest in
redemption, there lies the whole tragic story of Adam's
sin and judgment, of man's unceasing, unprofitable
labour, and of the coming of the Son of God to toil and
to give Himself until the lost position was recovered.

'My Father worketh even until now, and I work', He explained as He pursued His way. Only with the atoning price paid could He cry: 'It is finished!'

But because of that triumphant cry, the analogy we have drawn is a true one. Christianity indeed means that God has done everything in Christ, and that we simply step by faith into the enjoyment of that fact. Our key-word here is not of course, in its context, a command to 'sit down' but to see ourselves as 'seated' in Christ. Paul prays that the eyes of our heart may be enlightened (1. 18) to understand all that is contained for us in this double fact, that God has first by mighty power 'made him to sit', and then by grace 'made us to sit with him'. And the first lesson we must learn is this, that the work is not initially ours at all, but His. It is not that we work for God, but that He works for us. God *gives* us our position of rest. He brings His Son's finished work and presents it to us, and then He says to us, 'Please sit' (*ch'eng tso*). His offer to us cannot, I think, be better expressed than in the words of the invitation to the great banquet: 'Come; for all things are now ready' (Luke 14. 17). Our Christian life begins with the discovery of what God has provided.

## THE RANGE OF HIS FINISHED WORK

From this point onwards Christian experience proceeds as it began, not on the basis of our own work but always on that of the finished work of Another. Every new spiritual experience begins with an acceptance by faith of what God has done—with a new 'sitting down', if you like. This is a principle of life, and one which God Himself has appointed; and from beginning to end, each successive stage of the Christian life follows on the same divinely determined principle.

How can I receive the power of the Spirit for service?
Must I labour for it? Must I plead with God for it? Must
I afflict my soul by fastings and self-denials to merit it?
Never! That is not the teaching of Scripture. Think
again: How did we receive the forgiveness of our sins?
Paul tells us that it was 'according to the riches of his
grace', and that this was 'freely bestowed on us in the
Beloved' (1. 6, 7). We did nothing to merit it. We have
our redemption through His blood, that is, on the ground
of what *He* has done.

What, then, is God's basis for the outpouring of the
Spirit? It is the exaltation of the Lord Jesus (Acts 2. 33).
Because Jesus died on the Cross my sins are forgiven;
because He is exalted to the throne I am endued with
power from on high. The one gift is no more dependent
than the other upon what I am or what I do. I did not
merit forgiveness, and neither do I merit the gift of the
Spirit. I receive everything not by walking but by sitting
down, not by doing but by resting in the Lord. Hence,
just as there is no need to wait for the initial experience of
salvation, so there is no need to wait for the Spirit's outpouring. Let me assure you that you need not plead with
God for this gift, nor agonise, nor hold 'tarrying meetings'. It is yours not because of your doing but because
of the exaltation of Christ, 'in whom, having also believed, ye were sealed with the Holy Spirit of promise'.
This, no less than the forgiveness of sins, is contained in
'the gospel of your salvation' (1. 13).

Or consider another subject, one that is a special theme
of Ephesians. How do we become members of Christ?
What fits us to be parts of that Body which Paul speaks of
as 'the fulness of him'? Certainly we never arrive there
by walking. I am not joined to Him by effort of my own.
'There is one body and one Spirit, even as also ye were

called in one hope of your calling' (4. 4). Ephesians sets forth what *is*. It starts with Jesus Christ, and with the fact that God chose us *in Him* before the foundation of the world (1. 4). When the Holy Spirit shows us Christ and we believe on Him, then at once, with no further act on our part, there begins for us a life in union with Him.

But if all these things become ours by faith alone, what then of the now very urgent and practical matter of our sanctification? How can we know present deliverance from sin's reign? How is our 'old man', who has followed us and troubled us for years, to be 'crucified' and put away? Once again the secret is not in walking but in sitting; not in doing but in resting in something done. 'We *died* to sin.' We *'were baptized* . . . unto his death'. 'We *were buried* with him.' 'God . . . *quickened* us together with Christ.' (Rom. 6. 2, 3, 4; Eph. 2. 5.) All these statements are in the past (aorist) tense. Why is this? Because the Lord Jesus was crucified outside Jerusalem nearly two thousand years ago, and *I was crucified with Him*. This is the great historic fact. By it His experience has now become my spiritual history, and God can speak of me as already having everything 'with Him'. All that I now have I have 'with Christ'. In the Scriptures we never find these things spoken of as in the future, nor even to be desired in the present. They are historic facts of Christ, into which all we who have believed have entered.

'With Christ'—crucified, quickened, raised, set in the heavenlies: to the human mind these ideas are no less puzzling than were the words of Jesus to Nicodemus in John 3. 3. There it was a question of how to be born again. Here it is something even more improbable— something not only to be effected in us, as new birth, but to be seen and accepted as ours because it *has already been effected* long ago in Someone else. How could such a thing be? We cannot explain. We must receive it from God as something He has done. We were not born with Christ, but we were crucified with Him (Gal. 2. 20). Our union with Him began therefore with His death. God included us in Him there. We were 'with Him' because we were 'in Him'.

But how can I be sure that I am 'in Christ'? I can be sure because the Bible affirms that it is so, and that it was God who put me there. 'Of him [God] are ye in Christ Jesus' (1 Cor. 1. 30). 'He that stablisheth us with you in Christ . . . is God' (2 Cor. 1. 21). It is something accomplished by Him in His sovereign wisdom, to be seen, believed, accepted, and rejoiced in by us.

If I put a dollar note between the pages of a magazine, and then burn the magazine, where is the dollar note? It has gone the same way as the magazine—to ashes. Where the one goes the other goes too. Their history has become one. But, just as effectively, God has put us in Christ. What happened to Him happened also to us. All the experiences He met, we too have met *in Him*. 'Our old man was crucified with him, that the body of sin might be done away, that so we should no longer be in bondage to sin' (Rom. 6. 6). That is not an exhortation to struggle. That is history: our history, written in Christ before we were born. Do you believe that? It is true! Our crucifixion with Christ is a glorious historic fact. Our deliverance from sin is based, not on what we can do, nor even on what God is going to do for us, but on what He has already done for us in Christ. When that fact dawns upon us and we rest back upon it (Rom. 6. 11), then we have found the secret of a holy life.

But it is true that we know all too little of this in experience. Consider an example. If someone makes a very unkind remark about you in your presence, how do you

B

meet the situation? You compress your lips, clench your teeth, swallow hard, and take a firm grip upon yourself; and if with a great effort you manage to suppress all sign of resentment and be reasonably polite in return, you feel you have gained a great victory. But the resentment is still there; it has merely been covered up. And at times you do not even succeed in covering it. What is the trouble? The trouble is that you are trying to walk before you have sat down, and that way lies sure defeat. Let me repeat: no Christian experience begins with walking, but always with a definite sitting down. The secret of deliverance from sin is not to *do* something but to rest on what God has done.

An engineer living in a large city in the West left his homeland for the Far East. He was away for two or three years, and during his absence his wife was unfaithful to him and went off with one of his best friends. On his return home he found he had lost his wife, his two children and his best friend. At the close of a meeting which I was addressing, this grief-stricken man unburdened himself to me. 'Day and night for two solid years my heart has been full of hatred,' he said. 'I am a Christian, and I know I ought to forgive my wife and my friend, but though I try and try to forgive them, I simply cannot. Every day I resolve to love them, and every day I fail. What can I do about it?' 'Do nothing at all,' I replied. 'What do you mean?' he asked, startled. 'Am I to continue to hate them?' So I explained: 'The solution of your problem lies here, that when the Lord Jesus died on the Cross He not only bore your sins away but He bore *you* away too. When He was crucified, your old man was crucified in Him, so that that unforgiving "you", who simply cannot love those who have wronged you, has been taken right out of the way in His death. God has dealt with the whole situation in the Cross, and there is nothing left for you to deal with. Just say to Him, "Lord, I cannot love and I give up trying, but I count on Thy perfect love. I cannot forgive, but I trust Thee to forgive instead of me, and to do so henceforth in me." '

The man sat there amazed and said, 'That's all so new, I feel I must *do* something about it.' Then a moment later he added again, 'But what can I *do*?' 'God is waiting till you cease to do,' I said. 'When you cease doing, then God will begin. Have you ever tried to save a drowning man? The trouble is that his fear prevents him trusting himself to you. When that is so, there are just two ways of going about it. Either you must knock him unconscious and then drag him to the shore, or else you must leave him to struggle and shout until his strength gives way before you go to his rescue. If you try to save him while he has any strength left, he will clutch at you in his terror and drag you under, and both he and you will be lost. God is waiting for your store of strength to be utterly exhausted before He can deliver you. Once you have ceased to struggle, He will do everything. God is waiting for you to despair.'

My engineer friend jumped up. 'Brother,' he said, 'I've seen it. Praise God, it's all right now with me! There's nothing for me to do. *He* has done it all!' And with radiant face he went off rejoicing.


## God the Giver

Of all the parables in the Gospels, that of the prodigal son affords, I think, the supreme illustration of the way to please God. The father says: 'It was meet to make merry and be glad' (Luke 15. 32), and in these words Jesus reveals what it is that, in the sphere of redemption, supremely

rejoices His Father's heart. It is not an elder brother who
toils incessantly for the father, but a younger brother who
lets the father do everything for him. It is not an elder
brother who always wants to be the giver, but a younger
brother who is always willing to be the receiver. When
the prodigal returned home, having wasted his substance
in riotous living, the father had not a word of rebuke for
the waste nor a word of inquiry regarding the substance.
He did not sorrow over all that was spent; he only rejoiced over the opportunity the son's return afforded him
for spending more.

God is so wealthy that His chief delight is to give. His
treasure-stores are so full that it is pain to Him when we
refuse Him an opportunity of lavishing those treasures
upon us. It was the father's joy that he could find in the
prodigal an applicant for the robe, the ring, the shoes, and
the feast; it was his sorrow that in the elder son he found
no such applicant. It is a grief to the heart of God when
we try to provide things for Him. He is so very, very
rich. It gives Him true joy when we just let Him give and
give and give again to us. It is a grief to Him, too, when
we try to *do* things for Him, for He is so very, very able.
He longs that we will just let Him do and do and do. He
wants to be the Giver eternally, and He wants to be the
Doer eternally. If only we saw how rich and how great
He is, we would leave all the giving and all the doing to
Him.

Do you think that if you cease trying to please God
your good behaviour will cease? If you leave all the giving and all the working to God, do you think the result
will be less satisfactory than if you do some of it? It is
when we seek to do it ourselves that we place ourselves
back again under the Law. But the works of the Law,
even our best efforts are 'dead works', hateful to God be-

cause ineffectual. In the parable, both sons were equally far removed from the joys of the father's house. True, the elder son was not in the far country, yet he was only at home in theory. 'These many years do I serve thee, and yet . . .': his heart had not found rest. His theoretical position could never, as did the prodigal's, come to be enjoyed by him while he still clung to his own good works.

Just you stop 'giving', and you will prove what a Giver God is! Stop 'working', and you will discover what a Worker He is! The younger son was all wrong, but he came home and he found rest—and that is where Christian life begins. 'God, being rich in mercy, for his great love wherewith he loved us . . . made us to sit with him in the heavenly places, in Christ Jesus' (Eph. 2. 4, 6). 'It was meet to make merry and be glad!'

# 2

# WALK

We have sought to make it clear that Christian experience does not begin with walking but with sitting. Every time we reverse the divine order the result is disaster. The Lord Jesus has done everything for us, and our need now is to rest confidently in Him. He is seated in the throne, so we are carried through in His strength. It cannot be too strongly emphasised that all true spiritual experience begins from rest.

But it does not end there. Though the Christian life begins with sitting, sitting is always followed by walking. When once we have been well and truly seated and have found our strength in sitting down, then we do in fact begin to walk. Sitting describes our position with Christ in the heavenlies. Walking is the practical out-working of that heavenly position here on earth. As a heavenly people we are required to bear the stamp of that heavenliness upon us in our earthly conduct, and this raises new problems. What then, we must now ask, has Ephesians to say to us about walking? We shall find that the Epistle urges upon us two things. We will look now at the first of them.

'*I therefore, the prisoner in the Lord, beseech you to walk worthily of the calling wherewith ye were called, with all lowliness and meekness . . .*' (*4. 1, 2*).

'*This I say . . . that ye no longer walk as the Gentiles also walk, in the vanity of their mind . . . But . . . that ye be renewed in the spirit of your mind*' (*4. 17, 23*).

'*Walk in love, even as Christ also loved you, and gave himself up for you*' (5. 2, *mg.*).

'*Walk as children of light, . . . proving what is well-pleasing unto the Lord*' (5. 8, 10).

Eight times in Ephesians the word 'walk' is used. It means literally 'to walk around', and is used here figuratively by Paul to mean 'to deport oneself', 'to order one's behaviour'. It brings immediately before us the subject of Christian conduct, and the second section of the letter is largely taken up with this. But we saw earlier that the Body of Christ, the fellowship of Christian believers, is another great theme of Ephesians. Now, here in chapter 4, it is in view of such fellowship that we find this matter of a holy walk arises. Paul proceeds, in the light of our heavenly calling, to challenge us upon the whole field of our relationships, both domestic and public, addressing himself to neighbours, to husbands and wives, to parents and children, employers and employed, all in a most realistic way.

Let us be clear that the Body of Christ is not something remote and unreal, to be expressed only in heavenly terms. It is very present and practical, finding the real test of our conduct in our relations with others. For while it is true we are a heavenly people, it is no use just to talk of a distant heaven. Unless we bring heavenliness into our dwellings and offices, our shops and kitchens, and practise it there, it will be without meaning. May I suggest this, dear friends, that those who are parents and those who are children look through the New Testament to see what parents should be and children should be? We may be surprised, for I fear many of us who say we are seated in the heavenlies in Christ display a very questionable walk in our homes. And husbands too, and wives; there are quite a number of passages for them. Read Ephesians 5,

and then turn to 1 Corinthians 7. It would do every hus-
band and every wife good to read the latter chapter carefully to discover what a real married life—a spiritual one
before God and not just in theory—demands. You dare
not theorise about a thing that is so practical.

Look now, in the field of Christian relationships, how
forthright are the commands of God in the section here
before us. 'Walk . . . with longsuffering, forbearing one
another.' 'Putting away falsehood, speak ye truth each
one with his neighbour.' 'Be ye angry, and sin not.'
'Steal no more.' 'Let all bitterness . . . be put away from
you.' 'Be ye kind . . . forgiving each other.' 'Subjecting
yourselves to one another.' 'Provoke not.' 'Be obedient.'
'Forbear threatening.' Nothing could be more realistic
than this list of imperatives.

Let me remind you that the Lord Jesus Himself begins
His teaching on this very note. Notice carefully the
wording of this passage from His Sermon on the Mount:
'Ye have heard that it was said, An eye for an eye, and a
tooth for a tooth: but I say unto you, Resist not him that
is evil: but whosoever smiteth thee on thy right cheek,
turn to him the other also. And if any man would go to
law with thee, and take away thy coat, let him have thy
cloke also. And whosoever shall compel thee to go one
mile, go with him twain. Give to him that asketh thee,
and from him that would borrow of thee turn not thou
away. Ye have heard that it was said, Thou shalt love thy
neighbour, and hate thine enemy: but I say unto you,
Love your enemies, and pray for them that persecute you;
that ye may be sons of your Father which is in heaven:
for he maketh his sun to rise on the evil and the good, and
sendeth rain on the just and the unjust. For if ye love
them that love you, what reward have ye? do not even
the publicans the same? And if ye salute your brethren

only, what do ye more than others? do not even the Gentiles the same? Ye therefore shall be perfect, as your heavenly Father is perfect.' (Matt. 5. 38–48.)

'But,' you say, 'I cannot do it. These are impossible demands.' Maybe, like my engineer friend, you feel you have been wronged—perhaps terribly wronged—and you cannot bring yourself to forgive. *You* were in the right, and your enemy's action has been wholly unjust. To love him may be ideal, but it is impossible.

## THE PERFECTION OF THE FATHER

Since the day that Adam took the fruit of the tree of knowledge, man has been engaged in deciding what is good and what is evil. The natural man has worked out his own standards of right and wrong, justice and injustice, and striven to live by them. Of course as Christians we are different. Yes, but in what way are we different? Since we were converted a new sense of righteousness has been developed in us, with the result that we too are, quite rightly, occupied with the question of good and evil. But have we realised that for us the starting point is a different one? Christ is for us the Tree of Life. We do not begin from the matter of ethical right and wrong. We do not start from that other tree. We begin from *Him*; and the whole question for us is one of Life.

Nothing has done greater damage to our Christian testimony than our trying to be right and demanding right of others. We become preoccupied with what is and what is not right. We ask ourselves, Have we been justly or unjustly treated? and we think thus to vindicate our actions. But that is not our standard. The whole question for us is one of cross-bearing. You ask me, 'Is it right for someone to strike my cheek?' I reply, 'Of course not!

But the question is, do you only want to be right?' As Christians our standard of living can never be 'right or wrong', but the Cross. The principle of the Cross is our principle of conduct. Praise God that He makes His sun to shine on the evil and the good. With Him it is a question of His grace and not of right or wrong. But that is to be our standard also: 'Forgiving each other, even as God also in Christ forgave you' (4. 32). 'Right or wrong' is the principle of the Gentiles and tax gatherers. My life is to be governed by the principle of the Cross and of the perfection of the Father: 'Ye therefore shall be perfect, as your heavenly Father is perfect.'

A brother in South China had a rice field in the middle of the hill. In time of drought he used a water-wheel, worked by a tread-mill, to lift water from the irrigation stream into his field. His neighbour had two fields below his, and, one night, made a breach in the dividing bank and drained off all his water. When the brother repaired the breach and pumped in more water his neighbour did the same thing again, and this was repeated three or four times. So he consulted his brethren. 'I have tried to be patient and not to retaliate,' he said, 'but *is it right*?' After they had prayed together about it, one of them replied, 'If we only try to do the right thing, surely we are very poor Christians. We have to do something more than what is right.' The brother was much impressed. Next morning he pumped water for the two fields below, and in the afternoon pumped water for his own field. After that the water stayed in his field. His neighbour was so amazed at his action that he began to inquire the reason, and in course of time he too became a Christian.

So, my brethren, don't stand on your right. Don't feel that because you have gone the second mile you have done what is just. The second mile is only typical of the

third and the fourth. The principle is that of conformity
to Christ. We have nothing to stand for, nothing to ask or
demand. We have only to give. When the Lord Jesus died
on the Cross, He did not do so to defend our 'rights';
it was grace that took Him there. Now, as His children,
we try always to give others what is their due and more.

We have to remind ourselves that we are often *not* right.
We fail, and it is always good to learn from our failures—
to be ready to confess and willing to go beyond what is
necessary in doing so. The Lord wants this. Why? 'That
ye may be sons of your Father which is in heaven' (Matt.
5. 45). The question is one of practical sonship. True,
God has 'foreordained us unto adoption as sons through
Jesus Christ' (1. 5), but we make the mistake of thinking
that we have already 'come of age'—that we are already
mature sons. The Sermon on the Mount teaches us that
the children attain to the responsibility of sons in the
measure in which they manifest kinship of spirit and of
attitude with their Father. We are called to be 'perfect' in
love, showing forth His grace. So Paul also writes: 'Be
ye therefore imitators of God, as beloved children; and
walk in love, even as Christ also loved you, and gave himself up for you' (5. 1, 2, mg.).

We are faced with a challenge. Matthew 5 sets a standard that we may well feel is impossibly high, and Paul in
this section of Ephesians endorses it. The trouble is that
we just do not find in ourselves by nature the means to
attain to that standard—to walk 'as becometh saints'
(5. 3). Where, then, lies the answer to our problem of
God's exacting demands?

The secret is, in the words of Paul, 'the power that
worketh in us' (3. 20). In a parallel passage (Col. 1. 29)
he says: 'I labour also, striving according to his working,
which worketh in me mightily.'

We are back again in the first section of Ephesians. What is the secret strength of the Christian life? Whence has it its power? Let me give you the answer in a sentence: *The Christian's secret is his rest in Christ*. His power derives from his God-given position. All who sit can walk, for in the thought of God the one follows the other spontaneously. We sit for ever with Christ that we may walk continuously before men. Forsake for a moment our place of rest in Him, and immediately we are tripped and our testimony in the world is marred. But abide in Christ, and our position there ensures the power to walk worthy of Him here. If you desire an illustration of this kind of progress, think, first of all, not of a runner in a race but of a man in a car, or better still, of a cripple in a power-driven invalid carriage. What does he do? He *goes*—but he also *sits*. And he keeps going because he remains sitting. His progress follows from the position in which he has been placed. This, of course, is a far-from-perfect picture of the Christian life, but it may serve to remind us that our conduct and behaviour depend fundamentally upon our inward rest in Christ.

This explains Paul's language here. He has first learned to sit. He has come to a place of rest in God. As a result his walking is not based on his efforts but on God's mighty inward working. There lies the secret of his strength. Paul has seen himself seated in Christ; therefore his walk before men takes its character from Christ dwelling in him. Small wonder that he prays for the Ephesians: 'That Christ may dwell in your hearts through faith' (3. 17).

How does my wrist-watch go? By moving first, or by being moved? Of course it goes because first it is moved by a power outside itself. Then only will it do the work for which it was designed. And there are works for which we too are designed. 'We are his workmanship, created in

Christ Jesus for good works, which God afore prepared that we should walk in them' (2. 10). 'Work out your own salvation with fear and trembling,' writes Paul to the Philippians, 'for it is God which worketh in you both to will and to work, for his good pleasure.' God is working it in; work it out! That is the secret. But until we are willing for God to work it in, it is useless for us to try to work it out. Often we try to be meek and gentle without knowing what it means to let God work in us the meekness and gentleness *of Christ*. We try to show love, and, finding we have none, we ask the Lord for love. Then we are surprised that He does not seem to give it to us.

Let me take up again an earlier illustration. Perhaps there is a certain brother whom you find very trying and with whom you are constantly getting into difficulties. Whenever you meet him he says or does something calculated to arouse in you resentment. This troubles you. You say: 'I am a Christian and ought to love him. I want to love him; indeed I am *determined* to love him!' And so you pray very earnestly: 'Lord, increase my love for him. O God, give me love!' Then, taking a firm grip on yourself and summoning all your will-power, you set out with a genuine desire to display to him that love for which you have prayed. But alas, when you get into his presence something happens to bring all your good intentions to nought. His response to you is not in the least encouraging but rather the reverse, and immediately your old resentment flares up, and once again the utmost you can do is to be polite to him. Why is this? You were surely not *wrong* in seeking love from God? No, but you were wrong in seeking that love as something in itself, a kind of package-commodity, when what God desires is to express through you the love of His Son.

God has given us Christ. There is nothing now for us

to receive outside of Him.  The Holy Spirit has been sent
to produce what is of Christ in us; not to produce anything that is apart from or outside of Him.  We are
'strengthened with power through his Spirit in the inward
man; . . . to know the love of Christ' (3. 16, 19).  What we
show forth outwardly is what God has first put within.

Recall once again the great words of 1 Corinthians
1. 30.  Not only did God set us 'in Christ'.  By Him also
'Christ Jesus . . . was made unto us wisdom from God,
and righteousness and sanctification, and redemption.'
This is one of the grandest statements in Scripture.  *He*
'was made unto us . . .'.  If we believe this, we can put in
there anything we need, and can know that God has made
it good; for, through the Holy Spirit within us, the Lord
Jesus is Himself made unto us whatever we lack.  We
have been accustomed to look upon holiness as a virtue,
upon humility as a grace, upon love as a gift to be sought
from God.  But the Christ of God is *Himself* everything
that we shall ever need.

Many a time in my need I used to think of Christ as a
Person apart, and failed to identify Him in this practical
way with the 'things' I felt so strongly the lack of.  For
two whole years I was groping in that kind of darkness,
seeking to amass the virtues that I felt sure should make
up the Christian life, and getting nowhere in the effort.
And then one day—it was in the year 1933—light broke
from heaven for me, and I saw Christ ordained of God to
be made over to me in His fulness.  What a difference!
Oh the emptiness of 'things'!  Held by us out of relation
to Christ they are dead.  Once we see this it will be the
beginning of a new life for us.  Our holiness will be
spelled thereafter with a capital H, our love with a capital
L.  *He Himself* is revealed as the answer in us to all God's
demands.

Go back now to that difficult brother, but this time, before you go, address God thus: 'Lord, it is clear to me at last that in myself I cannot love him at all; but I know now that there is a life within me, the life of Thy Son, and that the law of that life is to love. It cannot but love him.' There is no need to exert yourself. Repose in Him. Count upon His life. Dare thus to go and see that brother and to speak to him—and here is the amazing thing! Quite unconsciously (and I would emphasise the word 'unconsciously', for the consciousness only comes afterwards) you find yourself speaking most pleasantly to him; quite unconsciously you love him; quite unconsciously you know him as your brother. You converse with him freely and in true fellowship, and on your return you find yourself saying with amazement: 'Why, I did not exercise the least bit of anxious care just now, and yet I did not become in the least bit irritable! In some unaccountable way the Lord was with me and His love triumphed.'

The operation of His life in us is in a true sense spontaneous, that is to say, it is without effort of ours. The all-important rule is not to 'try' but to 'trust', not to depend upon our own strength but upon His. For it is the flow of life which reveals what we truly are 'in Christ'. It is from the Fountain of life that the sweet water issues.

Too many of us are caught *acting* as Christians. The life of many Christians today is largely a pretence. They live a 'spiritual' life, talk a 'spiritual' language, adopt 'spiritual' attitudes, but they are doing the whole thing themselves. It is the effort involved that should reveal to them that something is wrong. They force themselves to refrain from doing this, from saying that, from eating the other, and how hard they find it all! It is just the same as when we Chinese try to talk a language that is not our own. No matter how hard we try, it does not come spontaneously;

we have to force ourselves to talk that way. But when it comes to speaking our own language, nothing could be easier. Even when we forget all about what we are doing, we still speak it. It flows. It comes to us perfectly naturally, and its very spontaneity reveals to everyone *what we are*.

Our life *is* the life of Christ, mediated in us by the indwelling Holy Spirit Himself, and the law of that life *is* spontaneous. The moment we see that fact we shall end our struggling and cast away our pretence. Nothing is so hurtful to the life of a Christian as acting; nothing so blessed as when our outward efforts cease and our attitudes become natural—when our words, our prayers, our very life, all become a spontaneous and unforced expression of the life within. Have we discovered how good the Lord is? Then *in us* He is as good as that! Is His power great? Then *in us* it is no less great! Praise God, His life is as mighty as ever, and in the lives of those who dare to believe the Word of God the divine life will be manifest in a power not one whit less mighty than was manifest of old.

What does our Lord mean when He says: 'Except your righteousness shall exceed the righteousness of the scribes and Pharisees, ye shall in no wise enter into the kingdom of heaven'? (Matt. 5. 20). We have seen above how He goes on to set the contrast between the requirements of the Law of Moses and His own tremendous demands, by His repeated use of the words: 'Ye have heard that it was said . . . but I say unto you . . .'. But since already, over many centuries, men had sought to attain to the first standard and had failed, how could the Lord dare to raise the standard higher still? He could do so only because He believed in His own life. He is not afraid of making the most exacting demands upon Himself. Indeed we may

well find comfort in reading the laws of the kingdom as
set forth in Matthew chapters 5 to 7, for they show what
utter confidence the Lord has in His own life *made available
to His children*. These three chapters set forth the divine
taxation of the divine life. The greatness of His demands
upon us only shows how confident He is that the resources
He has put within us are fully enough to meet them. God
does not command what He will not perform; but we
must throw ourselves back on Him for the performance.

Does some difficult situation confront us? Is it a problem of right or wrong, good or evil? We do not need to
look for wisdom. We need no longer apply to the tree of
knowledge. We have Christ, and *He* is made unto us
wisdom from God. The law of the Spirit of life in Christ
Jesus continually communicates to us His standards of
right and wrong, and, with them, the attitude of spirit
with which the difficult situation should be met.

More and more things will turn up to hurt our Christian
sense of righteousness and to test what our reactions are
going to be. We need to learn the principle of the Cross—
that our standard is not now the old but the new man
'which after God hath been created in righteousness and
holiness of truth' (4. 22–24). 'Lord, I've got no rights to
defend. Everything I have is through Thy grace, and
everything is in Thee!' I knew of an old Japanese Christian woman who was disturbed by a thief who had broken
into her house. In her simple but practical faith in the
Lord, she cooked the man a meal—then offered him her
keys. He was shamed by her action and God spoke to
him. Through her testimony that man is a brother in
Christ today.

Too many Christians have all the doctrine but live lives
that are a contradiction of it. They know all about chapters 1 to 3 of Ephesians but they do not put chapters 4 to 6

C

into practice. It were better to have no doctrine than to be a contradiction. Has God commanded something? Then throw yourself back on God for the means to do what He has commanded. May the Lord teach us that the whole principle of the Christian life is that we go beyond what is right to do that which is well-pleasing to Him.

## REDEEMING THE TIME

But there remains something further to be added to the above on the subject of our Christian walk. The word 'walk' has, as must already be obvious, a further meaning. It suggests first conduct or behaviour, but it also contains in it the idea of progress. To 'walk' is to 'proceed', to 'follow on', and we want to consider briefly now this further matter of our progress towards a goal.

'*Look therefore carefully how ye walk, not as unwise, but as wise; redeeming the time, because the days are evil. Wherefore be ye not foolish, but understand what the will of the Lord is*' (*5. 15–17*).

You will notice that in the above verses there is an association between the idea of Time and the difference between wisdom and foolishness. 'Walk . . . as wise; redeeming the time. . . . Be ye not foolish.' This is important. I want now to remind you of two other passages in which these things are similarly brought together:

'Then shall the kingdom of heaven be likened unto ten virgins. . . . Five of them were foolish, and five were wise. For the foolish, when they took their lamps, took no oil with them. . . . But at midnight there is a cry, Behold, the bridegroom! Come ye forth to meet him. Then all those virgins arose, and trimmed their lamps. And the foolish said, . . . Our lamps are going out. . . . And while they went away to buy, the bridegroom came; and they that

were ready went in with him to the marriage feast: and
the door was shut. Afterward come also the other virgins . . .' (see Matt. 25. 1–13).

'And I saw, and behold, the Lamb standing on the
mount Zion, and with him a hundred and forty and four
thousand, having his name and the name of his Father,
written on their foreheads. . . . These are virgins. These
are they which follow the Lamb whithersoever he goeth.
These were purchased from among men, to be the firstfruits unto God and unto the Lamb. And in their mouth
was found no lie: they are without blemish' (see Rev.
14. 1–5).

There are many passages of Scripture that assure us that
what God has begun He will finish. Our Saviour is a
Saviour to the uttermost. No Christian believer will be
'half-saved' at the end, even if now that might be said of
us in any sense. God will perfect every man who has faith
in Him. That is what we believe, and we must keep it in
mind as a background for what we are going to say next.
With Paul, we are 'confident of this very thing, that he
which began a good work in you will perfect it until the
day of Jesus Christ' (Phil. 1. 6). There are no limits to
God's power. He 'is able . . . to set you before the presence of his glory without blemish' (Jude 24; and see:
2 Tim. 1. 12; Eph. 3. 20).

It is, however, when we turn to the subjective aspect of
this—to its practical outworking in our lives here and
now on the earth—that we encounter the question of
Time. In Revelation 14 there are firstfruits (verse 4) and
there is a harvest (verse 15). What is the difference between harvest and firstfruits? It is certainly not one of
quality, for the whole crop is one. Their difference lies
only in the time of their ripeness. Some fruits reach
maturity before others and thus they become 'firstfruits'.

My home town in Fukien province is famous for its oranges. I would say (and no doubt I am prejudiced!) that there are none like them anywhere in the world. As you look out on the hills at the beginning of the orange season, all the groves are green. But if you look more carefully you will see, sprinkled here and there on the trees, golden oranges already showing up. It is a beautiful sight to see the flecks of gold dotted among the dark green trees. Later the whole crop will ripen and the groves will turn to gold, but now it is these firstfruits that are gathered. They are carefully hand-picked, and it is they that fetch the top market-prices—often three times the price of the harvest.

All will reach ripeness, somehow. But the Lamb is seeking firstfruits. The 'wise' in the parable are not those who have done better, but those who have done well *at an earlier hour*. The others, be it noted, were also virgins— 'foolish', no doubt, but not false. Along with the wise, they had gone out to meet the Bridegroom. They too had oil in their lamps, and their lamps were burning. But they had not reckoned on His tarrying, and now that their lamps burned low they had no reserve of oil in their vessels, nor had the others enough to spare them.

Some are troubled at this point by the Lord's words to the foolish ones: 'I know you not.' How, they feel, could He say this of them if they represent His true children, 'espoused . . . as a pure virgin to Christ'? (2 Cor. 11. 2). But we must recognise the whole point of the teaching of this parable, which is surely that there is some privilege of serving Him in the future which His children may miss by being unprepared. It says that the five came to the door and said: 'Lord, Lord, open to us.' What door? Certainly not the door of salvation. If you are lost, you cannot come to the door of heaven and knock. When therefore the Lord says: 'I know you not, 'He surely uses these words in some such limited sense as in the following illustration.

In Shanghai the son of a police-court magistrate was taken up for careless driving. He was brought to court and found his father sitting on the magistrate's bench. Court procedure is more or less the same the world over, and so the boy was asked: 'What is your name? What is your address? What is your occupation?' and so on. Astonished, he turned to his father: 'Father, do you mean to say you don't know me?' Rapping on his desk the father answered sternly: 'Young man, I do not know you. What is your name? What is your address?' He did not of course mean by this that he did not know him at all. In the family and in the home he knew him, but *in that place and at that time* he did not know him. Though still his father's son, the boy must go right through the court procedure and pay his fine.

Yes, all ten virgins had oil in their lamps. What distinguished the foolish was that they had no reserve in their vessels. As true Christians, they have life in Christ, and they have a testimony before men. But theirs is a fitful testimony for they live a hand-to-mouth existence. They have the Spirit, but they are not, we may say, 'filled with the Spirit'. When the crisis comes they must go out to buy more oil. In the end, of course, all the ten had enough. But the difference lay in the fact that the wise had sufficient oil in time, while the foolish, when at length they did have sufficient, had missed the purpose for which it was intended. It is all a question of time, and this is the point which the Lord seeks to drive home when, at the end of the parable, he urges his disciples not just to be disciples but to be watchful disciples.

'Be not drunken with wine, wherein is riot, but be filled

with the Spirit' (5. 18). In Matthew 25 it is not a question
of the initial reception of Jesus Christ, nor yet of the coming of the Holy Spirit upon His servants for spiritual gifts.
It is a question of the extra oil in the vessel—of the light
being sustained, through however long a time of waiting,
by means of the continual miraculous supply of the Spirit
within (for whereas in the parable there is both a lamp and
a vessel, in reality we are the lamp and we are the vessel).
What Christian could possibly live in eternity in heaven
without knowing this inner fulness? Surely not one
virgin can escape this? And so the Lord is taking all possible steps to bring us to the knowledge of that fulness
now. 'Watch therefore, for ye know not the day nor the
hour.'

'Be being filled' (*plerousthe*) is the unusual expression
used here in relation to the Holy Spirit. 'Allow yourselves
to be continually made full.' It is not a crisis, as at Pente-
cost, but a state we are to be in all the time. And it is not
something external, but internal; not a question of spiritual gifts and manifestations outwardly but of the personal presence and activity of the Holy Spirit within our
spirits, guaranteeing that the light in the vessel will burn
undimmed, long after midnight if need be.

And moreover, it is not wholly a personal thing. As
the next verse (5. 19) surely indicates, it is something
which we share with other Christians in mutual dependence. For to be 'filled with the Spirit' means, in the language of that verse, not merely 'singing and making
melody with your heart to the Lord' but '*speaking one to
another* in psalms and hymns and spiritual songs'. Some
of us may well find it easy to sing solos, but much harder
to sing in time and harmony as a quartet or even as a duet.
Yet this message of oneness in the Spirit lies at the heart
of our second section of Ephesians (see 4. 3, 15, 16). The

fulness of the Spirit is given to us that we should sing
*together* a new song before the throne (Rev. 14. 3).

But, to keep to our main emphasis, let me repeat that
folly or wisdom hinges on this one point alone, that if you
are wise you will seek this fulness sooner, but if you are
foolish you will put it off till later. Some of us are parents
and have children. How greatly those children can differ
in temperament! One will obey at once; another will
think that by procrastination he can avoid the need to do
so. If that is indeed the case, and you are weak enough to
allow him a loophole for escape, then the one who pro-
crastinates is in fact the wise one, for he succeeds in doing
nothing. But if your word holds, if your command cannot
be evaded and ultimately *must* be obeyed, then he is certainly the wiser who faces the issue squarely at once.

Get clear about the will of God. If God's words can be
discounted, then you might not be foolish to try to escape
their implications; but if God is an unchanging God with
an unchanging will, then be wise; redeem the time. Seek
above all things to have that extra supply of oil in the
vessel, 'that ye may be filled unto all the fulness of God'
(3. 19).

The parable does not answer all our questions. How
do the foolish buy? We are not told. We are nowhere
told what further steps God may have to take to bring all
His children eventually to maturity. That is not our con-
cern. We are concerned here with firstfruits. We are
being urged to press on; not to speculate on what may
happen if we don't.

You cannot, by dodging the issue, avoid reaching
maturity—or paying the price of it. But wisdom is con-
nected with time. Those who are wise redeem the time.
Just as my fountain pen is now filled and ready to my
hand for immediate use, so, by co-operating with the

Lord, the wise provide God with what He wants: handy
tools, instantly available to Him.

Look at the apostle Paul. He is consumed with a burning passion. He has seen that God's purpose for us is
bound up with the 'fulness of the times' (1. 10). He is one
of those who have 'before hoped in Christ' by resting in
a salvation that is yet to be fully revealed 'in the ages to
come' (1. 12; 2. 7). And in view of all this, what does he
do? He walks. And he not only walks; he runs. 'I therefore so run, as not uncertainly' (1 Cor. 9. 26). 'I press on
toward the goal unto the prize of the high calling of God
in Christ Jesus' (Phil. 3. 14).

Often when souls come into an understanding of
spiritual things and begin to go on with the Lord, the
feeling in my heart is: 'Oh, if only they had come to see
this five years earlier!' The time is so short, even if we
*are* going on. There is such need for urgency. For remember, it is not a question of what we get out of it. It
is a question of *what the Lord must have now*. The Lord's
need today is for ready instruments. Why? 'Because the
days are evil.' The situation is desperate among the Christian public. Oh that we might see it!

The Lord may have to deal drastically with us. Paul
had to say 'I am an abortive child'. He had passed through
tremendous crises to bring him to the point where he then
was—and still he pressed on. It is always a question of
time. God may have to do something in us swiftly, com-
pressing it into a short space; but He *has* to do that much.
May the eyes of our heart be enlightened to know what
is 'the hope of his calling', and then may we walk—nay,
run—as those who 'understand what the will of the Lord
is' (1. 18; 5. 17). The Lord always loved desperate souls.

# 3
# STAND

*'Finally, be strong in the Lord, and in the strength of his might. Put on the whole armour of God, that ye may be able to stand against the wiles of the devil. . . . That ye may be able to withstand in the evil day, and, having done all, to stand. Stand therefore, having girded your loins . . . having put on the breast-plate . . . having shod your feet . . . taking up the shield . . . and the helmet . . . and the sword . . . praying . . . and watching'* (6. 10–11, 13–18).

Christian experience begins with sitting and leads to walking, but it does not end with these. Every Christian must learn also to stand. Each one of us must be prepared for the conflict. We must know how to sit with Christ in heavenly places and we must know how to walk worthy of Him down here, but we must also know how to stand before the foe. This matter of conflict now comes before us in the third section of Ephesians (6. 10–20). It is what Paul calls 'our wrestling with wicked spirits'.

But let us first remind ourselves once again of the order in which Ephesians presents us with these things. It is: 'sit . . . walk . . . stand'. For no Christian can hope to enter the warfare of the ages without learning first to rest in Christ and in what He has done, and then, through the strength of the Holy Spirit within, to follow Him in a practical, holy life here on earth. If he is deficient in either of these he will find that all the talk about spiritual warfare remains only talk; he will never know its reality.

Satan can afford to ignore him for he does not count for
anything. Yet the very same Christian can be made
strong 'in the Lord, and in the strength of his might' by
knowing the values first of His exaltation and then of His
indwelling (compare 6. 10 with 1. 19 and 3. 16). It is with
these two lessons well and truly learned that he comes to
appreciate the third principle of the Christian life now
summed up in the word 'Stand'.

God has an arch-enemy, and under his power are count-
less demons and fallen angels seeking to overrun the
world with evil and to exclude God from His own kingdom. This is the meaning of verse 12. It is an explanation
of things taking place around us. *We* see only 'flesh and
blood' ranged against us—that is to say, a world system of
hostile kings and rulers, sinners and evil men. No, says
Paul, our wrestling is not against these, 'but against the
principalities, against the powers, against the world-rulers
of this darkness, against the spiritual hosts of wickedness
in the heavenly places'—in short against the wiles of the
devil himself. Two thrones are at war. God is claiming
the earth for His dominion, and Satan is seeking to usurp
the authority of God. The Church is called to displace
Satan from his present realm and to make Christ Head
over all. What are we doing about it?

I want now to deal with this matter of our warfare first
in general terms in relation to our personal Christian lives
and then in a more special sense in relation to the work of
the Lord entrusted to us. There are many direct assaults
of Satan upon God's children. Of course we must not
attribute to the devil those troubles that are the result of
our own breach of divine laws. We should, by now,
know how to put these right. But there are physical attacks upon the saints, attacks of the evil one upon their
bodies and minds, of which we must take serious account.

Surely, too, there are few of us who do not know something of the enemy's assaults upon our spiritual life. Are
we going to let these pass unchallenged?

We have our position with the Lord in the heavenlies,
and we are learning how to walk with Him before the
world; but how are we to acquit ourselves in the presence
of the adversary—His adversary and ours? God's word
is: 'Stand!' 'Put on the whole armour of God that you
may be able to stand against the wiles of the devil.' The
Greek verb 'stand' with its following preposition
'against' in verse 11 really means 'hold your ground'.
There is a precious truth hidden in that command of God.
It is not a command to invade a foreign territory. Warfare, in modern parlance, would imply a command to
'march'. Armies march into other countries to occupy and
to subdue. God has not told us to do this. We are not to
march but to stand. The word 'stand' implies that the
ground disputed by the enemy is really His, and therefore
ours. We need not struggle to gain a foothold on it.

Nearly all the weapons of our warfare described in
Ephesians are purely defensive. Even the sword can be
used as well for defence as for offence. The difference between defensive and offensive warfare is this, that in the
former I have got the ground and only seek to keep it,
whereas in the latter I have not got the ground and am
fighting in order to get it. And that is precisely the difference between the warfare waged by the Lord Jesus and
the warfare waged by us. His was offensive; ours is, in
essence, defensive. He warred against Satan in order to
gain the victory. Through the Cross He carried that warfare to the very threshold of Hell itself, to lead forth
thence his captivity captive (4. 8, 9). Today we war
against Satan only to maintain and consolidate the victory
which He has already gained. By the resurrection God

proclaimed His Son Victor over the whole realm of darkness, and the ground Christ won He has given to us. We
do not need to fight to obtain it. We only need to hold it
against all challengers.

Our task is one of holding, not of attacking. It is a
matter not of advance but of sphere, the sphere of Christ.
In the person of Jesus Christ, God has already conquered.
He has given us His victory to *hold*. Within the sphere of
Christ the enemy's defeat is already a fact, and the Church
has been put there to keep him defeated. Satan is the one
who must do the counter-attacking in his efforts to dis-
lodge us from that sphere. For our part we need not
struggle to occupy ground that is already ours. In Christ
we *are* conquerors—nay, 'more than conquerors' (Rom.
8. 37). In Him, therefore, we *stand*. Thus today we do not
fight *for* victory; we fight *from* victory. We do not fight
in order to win but because in Christ we have already
won. Overcomers are those who rest in the victory already given to them by their God.

When you fight *to get* the victory, then you have lost
the battle at the very outset. Suppose Satan sets out to
assault you in your home or in your business. Difficulties
mount up, misunderstandings arise, a situation that you
can neither deal with nor escape threatens to overwhelm
you. You pray, you fast, you struggle and resist for days,
but nothing happens. Why? You are trying to fight into
victory, and in doing so are relinquishing to the enemy
the very ground that is yours. For victory is still for you a
distant thing, somewhere ahead of you, and you cannot
reach it. I was in just such a situation once myself, and
God brought to my mind the word in 2 Thessalonians
concerning the man of sin, whom the Lord Jesus 'shall
slay with the breath of his mouth'. The thought came:
It will need but a breath from my Lord to finish him off,

and here am I trying to raise a hurricane! Was not Satan
once for all defeated? Then this victory too is already
won.

Only those who sit can stand. Our power for standing,
as for walking, lies in our having first been made to sit
together with Christ. The Christian's walk and warfare
alike derive their strength from his position there. If he
is not sitting before God he cannot hope to stand before
the enemy.

Satan's primary object is not to get us to sin, but
simply to make it easy for us to do so by getting us off
the ground of perfect triumph on to which the Lord has
brought us. Through the avenue of the head or of the
heart, through our intellect or our feelings, he assaults our
rest in Christ or our walk in the Spirit. But for every
point of his attack defensive armour is provided, the helmet and the breastplate, the girdle and the shoes, while
over all is the shield of faith to turn aside his fiery darts.
Faith says: Christ is exalted. Faith says: We are saved by
His grace. Faith says: We have access through Him.
Faith says: He indwells us by His Spirit (see 1.20; 2. 8;
3. 12, 17).

Because victory is His, therefore it is ours. If only we
will not try to gain the victory but simply to maintain it,
then we shall see the enemy utterly routed. We must not
ask the Lord to enable *us* to overcome the enemy, nor
even look to *Him* to overcome, but praise Him because
He has already done so; He *is* Victor. It is all a matter o
faith in Him. If we believe the Lord, we shall not pray so
much but rather we shall praise Him more. The simpler
and clearer our faith in Him, the less we shall pray in such
situations and the more we shall praise.

Let me say again: In Christ we *are already* conquerors.
Is it not obvious then that, since this is so, for us merely

to pray for victory—unless that prayer is shot through
with praise—must be to court defeat by throwing away
our fundamental position? Let me ask you: Has defeat
been your experience? Have you found yourself hoping
that one day you will be strong enough to win? Then my
prayer for you can go no further than that of the apostle
Paul to his Ephesian readers. It is that God may open
your eyes anew to see yourself seated with Him who has
Himself been made to sit 'far above all rule, and authority,
and power, and dominion, and every name that is named'
(1. 20, 21). The difficulties around you may not alter; the
lion may roar as loudly as ever; but you need no longer
*hope* to overcome. In Christ Jesus you *are* victor in the
field.

## In His Name

But this is not all. Ephesians 6 is concerned with more
than the personal side of our warfare. It has to do too
with the work of God entrusted to us—the utterance of
the mystery of the Gospel of which Paul has already had
much to say (see 3. 1–13). For this it arms us now with
the sword of the Word and its companion weapon,
prayer.

'*Take . . . the sword of the Spirit, which is the word of God:
with all prayer and supplication praying at all seasons in the
Spirit, and watching thereunto in all perseverance and supplication for all the saints, and on my behalf, that utterance may be
given unto me in opening my mouth, to make known with boldness
the mystery of the gospel, for which I am an ambassador in chains;
that in it I may speak boldly, as I ought to speak*' (6. 17–20).

I want to say something more about this warfare in its
relation to our work for God, for here we may encounter
a difficulty. It is true, on the one hand, that our Lord

Jesus is seated 'far above all rule, and authority', and that all things have been put 'in subjection under his feet' (1. 21, 22). Clearly it is in the light of this completed victory that we are to 'give thanks always for all things *in the name of Jesus Christ*' (5. 20). Yet on the other hand we have to admit that we do not yet see all things subject to Him. There are still, as Paul says, hosts of wicked spirits in the heavenly places, dark, evil powers behind this world's rulers, occupying territory that is rightly His. How far are we correct in calling this a defensive warfare? We do not want to be falsely presumptive. When, therefore, and under what conditions are we justified in occupying territory that is outwardly the enemy's and holding it in the name of the Lord Jesus?

Let us 'take ... the word of God' to help us here. What does it tell us about prayer and action 'in the name'? Consider first the following two passages: 'Verily I say unto you, What things soever ye shall bind on earth shall be bound in heaven: and what things soever ye shall loose on earth shall be loosed in heaven. Again I say unto you, that if two of you shall agree on earth as touching anything that they shall ask, it shall be done for them ... For where two or three are gathered together in my name, there am I. ...' (Matt. 18. 18–20). 'In that day ye shall ask me nothing. Verily, verily, I say unto you, If ye shall ask anything of the Father, he will give it you in my name. Hitherto have ye asked nothing in my name: ask, and ye shall receive, that your joy may be fulfilled. ... In that day ye shall ask in my name' (John 16. 23, 24, 26).

None can be saved without knowing the name of Jesus, and none can be effectively used of God without knowing the authority of that name. The apostle Paul makes it clear that the 'name' to which Jesus alludes in the above passages is not simply the name by which He was known while here among men. To be sure, it *is* that very self-same name of His humanity, but it is that name invested now with the title and authority given to Him by God after He had become obedient to death (Phil. 2. 6–10). It is the outcome of His sufferings, the name of His exaltation and glory; and today it is in *that* 'name which is above every name' that we gather and that we ask of God.

This distinction is made not by Paul alone but already by Jesus Himself in the second passage quoted above: 'Hitherto ye have asked nothing . . . In that day ye shall ask' (verses 24, 26). For the disciples 'that day' will differ greatly from the 'now' of verse 22. Something they do not have now they will receive then, and having received it they will use it. That something is the authority that goes with His name.

Our eyes must be opened to see the mighty change wrought by the ascension. The name of Jesus certainly establishes the identity of the One in the throne with the Carpenter of Nazareth, but it goes further than that. It represents now the power and dominion given to Him by God, a power and a dominion before which every knee in heaven and earth and beneath the earth must bow. Even the Jewish leaders recognised that there could be this kind of significance in a mere name, when they inquired of the disciples concerning the healing of the lame man: 'By what power, or in what name, have ye done this?' (Acts 4. 7).

Today the name tells us that God has committed all authority to His Son, so that in the very name itself there is power. But further, we must note in Scripture the recurring expression '*in* the name'—that is to say, the use to which the apostles in fact put that name. It is not only that He *has* such a name, but that we are to *use* it. In three passages in His last discourse the Lord Jesus repeats the words 'ask in my name' (see John 14. 13, 14; 15. 16; 16. 23–26). He has placed that authority in our hands for us to use. Not only is it His, but it is 'given among men' (Acts 4. 12). If we do not know our part in it we suffer great loss.

The power of His name operates in three directions. In our preaching it is effective to the salvation of men (Acts 4. 10–12) through the remission of their sins, and through their cleansing, justification, and sanctification to God (Luke 24. 47; Acts 10. 43; 1 Cor. 6. 11). In our warfare it is mighty against the Satanic powers, to bind and bring them into subjection (Mark 16. 17; Luke 10. 17–19; Acts 16. 18). And as we have already seen, in our asking it is effective towards God, for twice we are told: 'Whatsoever ye shall ask . . .', and twice: 'If ye shall ask anything . . .' (John 14. 13, 14; 15. 16; 16. 23). Faced with these challenging words, well might we reverently say: 'Lord, Your courage is very great!'

For God thus to commit Himself to His servants is indeed a tremendous thing. Glance now with me at three incidents in the Acts which serve to illustrate this further: 'Peter said, . . . In the name of Jesus Christ of Nazareth, walk' (Acts 3. 6). 'Paul . . . turned and said to the spirit, I charge thee in the name of Jesus Christ to come out of her. And it came out that very hour' (Acts 16. 18). 'Certain . . . exorcists, took upon them to name over them which had the evil spirits the name of the Lord Jesus, saying, I adjure you by Jesus whom Paul preacheth. . . . And the evil spirit answered and said unto them, Jesus I know, and Paul I know; but who are ye?' (Acts 19. 13, 15).

Observe first the action of Peter in dealing with the crippled man at the gate. He does not kneel and pray and

D

ask the mind of the Lord first. At once he says: 'Walk.' He uses the name as if it were his to use, not something far away in heaven. With Paul at Philippi it is the same. He senses in his spirit that the Satanic activity has gone far enough. We are not told that thereupon he pauses to pray. No, his is a true walk before God, and because this is so he can, as a custodian of the name, take action almost as though the power were in himself. He commands, and the evil spirit flees 'that very hour'.

What is this? It is an example of what I shall call God's 'committal' of Himself to man. God has committed Himself to His servants to act through them, as they take action 'in the name'. And they, what do they do? It is clear that they do nothing of themselves. They use the name. Equally clearly no other name, whether their own or that of another apostle, will have the same effect. All that takes place results from the impact of the name of the Lord Jesus on the situation, and *they are authorised to use that name*.

God looks at His Son in the glory, not at us here on the earth. It is because He sees us seated with Him *there* that His name and His authority can be entrusted to us here. A simple illustration will help to make this clear. Some time ago my fellow-worker sent to me for a sum of money. I read his letter, prepared what he had asked, and gave the sum to the messenger. Was I right? Yes, certainly. The letter bore my friend's signature, and to me that was sufficient. Should I instead have asked the messenger *his* name and age and employment and native place, and then perhaps sent him away because I objected to what *he* was? No, by no means; for he had come in my friend's name, and I honoured that name.

## The Divine Self-committal

It is a mighty thing that God has done in thus committing Himself to His Church. In so doing He has entrusted to His servants the greatest possible power; that of One whose dominion is 'above every name that is named, not only in this world, but also in that which is to come' (1. 21). Jesus is now exalted in heaven, and all His work of saving men, speaking to their hearts, and working for them miracles of His grace, is done through the medium of His servants as they act *in His name*. Thus the Church's work is His work. The name of Jesus is in fact God's greatest legacy to her, for where such a self-committal of God is really operative, He Himself takes responsibility for what is done in that name. And God *desires* so to commit Himself, for He has allowed Himself no other means for completing His task.

No work is worthy to be called a work of God if God is not, in this sense, committing Himself to it. It is the authorisation to use His name that counts. We must be able to stand up and speak *in His name*. If not, our work lack spiritual impact. But let me tell you, this is not something that can be 'worked up' at a time of crisis. It is a fruit of obedience to God and of a resulting spiritual position known and maintained. It is something we must have already if it is to be available in a time of need.

'Jesus I know, and Paul I know.' Praise God for the second! The evil powers recognise the Son; the Gospels give us plenty of evidence of this. But there are those also who are in union with the Son, and they too count in Hades. The question is, *Can* God commit Himself thus to you?

Let me illustrate again. If something is to be done in my name, it means that, subject to certain conditions, I give my name to another to use, and that I am then prepared to take responsibility for what he does with it. It may mean, for example, that I give him my cheque book and my signature. Of course, if I am poor, with no personal standing and no bank account, my name is of little moment. I well remember how, as a student, I used to be fond of stamping my name everywhere, on books, papers, and anything that came to hand. But when I first had a cheque book and a bank account—fourteen dollars in the Post Office—I became very careful over the use of my personal seal, for fear someone else should counterfeit it and use it.* My name had become important to me.

How powerful and how wealthy is our Lord Jesus! How precious to Him is His name! If, therefore, He is to take responsibility for everything that happens in consequence, how careful must He be as to how that name is used! I ask you again: *Can* God commit Himself—His 'bank balance', His 'cheque book', His 'signature'—to *you*? That question must be settled first. Then only can you use His name freely. Then only 'what things soever ye shall bind on earth shall be bound in heaven'. Then, because of the reality of His committal to you, you can move as a true representative of Him in this world. That is the fruit of union with Him.

Are we in such a union with the Lord that He *will* thus commit Himself to what we are doing? It seems often that we shall be running a big risk in stepping into a situation with only the promises of God to back up our stand. The point is, will God—*can* God—back us up?

* The Chinese custom is for everyone to have his own personal *tu-cheng*, a seal or die bearing the characters of his name carved in wood, stone or ivory in an individual design. The impression is usually made with an opaque red ink. This is felt to be less easily forged than a hand-written signature, and the seal is kept under lock and key and used for signing cheques and other personal documents.—ED.

Briefly let me outline four essential features of a work to which God can fully commit Himself. The first vital need is of a true revelation to our hearts of the eternal purpose of God. We cannot do without this. If I am working on a building, even as an unskilled labourer, I must know whether the objective is a garage or an aeroplane hangar or a palace. I must see the plan or I cannot be an intelligent worker. Today evangelism is assumed by most Christians to be *the* work of God. But evangelism can never be an unrelated thing. It must be integrated with God's whole plan, for it is in fact but a means to an end. That end is the pre-eminence of the Son of God, and evangelism is bringing in the sons among whom He shall stand pre-eminent.

In Paul's generation every believer had a specific relation to the eternal purpose of God (see especially chapter 4. 11–16). That should be no less true of us today. The eyes of God are turning towards His coming kingdom. What we know as organised Christianity will shortly have to make way for something else—the sovereign rule of Christ. But as with the kingdom of Solomon, so now, there is first a period of spiritual warfare represented by the reign of David. God is seeking those who will co-operate with Him today in that preparatory warfare.

It is a question of the identification of my purpose with the eternal purpose of God. All Christian work that is not so identified is fragmentary and unrelated, and it does not ultimately get anywhere. We have to seek from God a revelation to our hearts by His Holy Spirit of 'the counsel of his will' (see 1. 9–12) and then to ask ourselves concerning the work to which we are going back after reading this: 'Is it directly related to that?' When that is settled, all the small questions of daily guidance will solve themselves.

Secondly, all work that is going to be effective in the divine purpose must be conceived by God. If *we* plan work and then ask God to bless it, we need not expect God to commit Himself to it. God's name can never be a 'rubber-stamp' to authorise work that is ours in conception. True, there may be blessing upon such work, but it will be partial and not full. There can be no 'in His name' there; only, alas, our name!

'The Son can do nothing of himself.' How often in the book of the Acts we find the Holy Spirit's prohibitions! We read in chapter 16 how Paul and those with him were 'forbidden of the Holy Ghost to speak the word in Asia'. And again: 'The Spirit of Jesus suffered them not.' Yet this book is the book of the *acts* of the Holy Spirit, not of His 'inactivities'. Too often we think that the actual doing is what matters. We have to learn the lesson of not doing—of keeping quiet for Him. We have to learn that if God does not move we dare not move. When we have learned this, then it is that He can safely send us forth to speak for Him.

I must have, therefore, a knowledge of God's will in my particular sphere of work. Out of that knowledge only should the work be initiated. The abiding principle of all true Christian work is: 'In the beginning God . . .'

Thirdly, all work to be effective must depend for its continuance upon the power of God alone. What is power? We often use the word loosely. We say of a man, 'He is a very powerful speaker', but we have to ask ourselves the question: What power is he using? Is it spiritual power or is it natural power? There is today all too much place given to the power of nature in the service of God. We have got to learn that, even where God has initiated a work, if we are trying to accomplish it in our own power God will never commit Himself to it.

You ask me what I mean by natural power. Put very simply, it is what we can do without the help of God. We give a man the task of organising something—of planning a Gospel campaign or some other Christian activity —because he is naturally a good organiser. But if that is so, how hard will he pray? If he is accustomed to depend on his natural gifts, he may feel no need to cry to God. The trouble with us all is that there are so many things we can do without relying upon God. We must be brought to the place where, naturally gifted though we may be, we dare not act, we dare not speak, except in conscious and continual dependence on Him.

Stephen described Moses, after his Egyptian education, as a man 'mighty in his words and works'. Yet, after God had dealt with him, Moses had to say: 'Oh Lord, I am not eloquent, neither heretofore nor since thou hast spoken to thy servant: for I am slow of speech, and of a slow tongue.' When a born orator comes to the place of saying 'I can't speak', then he has learned a fundamental lesson and is on the road to real usefulness for God. That discovery involves a crisis and then a lifelong process, both of them implied, surely, in Luke's expression 'baptised into the name' (Acts 8. 16; 19. 5). That expression points every new believer to the necessity for a fundamental knowledge of the death and resurrection of Christ in its relation to his entire natural man. Somehow, in our history with God, we must experience that initial crippling touch of His hand to weaken our natural strength, so that we stand forth on the ground of resurrection life in Christ alone, where death has no longer any claim. After that the circle goes on widening, as fresh areas of our own self-energy are brought under the working of the Cross. The way is a costly one, but it is God's sure way to fruitfulness of life and ministry, for it provides Him

with the ground He requires in order that He may give
His backing to what we do in the name of His Son.

In the work of God today things are often so consti-
tuted that we have no need to rely upon God. But the
Lord's verdict upon all such work is uncompromising:
'Apart from me ye can do nothing.' Such work as man
can do apart from God is wood, hay, stubble, and the test
of fire will prove it so. For divine work can only be done
with divine power, and that power is to be found in the
Lord Jesus alone. It is made available to us in Him on
the resurrection side of the Cross. That is to say, it is
when we have reached the point where in all honesty we
cry: 'I cannot speak,' that we discover God *is* speaking.
When we come to an end of our works, His work begins.
Thus the fire in the days to come and the Cross today
effect the same thing. What cannot stand the Cross today
will not survive the fire later. If *my* work, which is done
in *my* power is brought to death, how much comes out of
the grave? Nothing! Nothing ever survives the Cross
but what is wholly of God in Christ.

God never asks us to do anything we *can* do. He asks
us to live a life which we can never live and to do a work
which we can never do. Yet, by His grace, we *are* living
it and doing it. The life we live is the life of Christ lived
in the power of God, and the work we do is the work of
Christ carried on through us by His Spirit whom we
obey. Self is the only obstruction to that life and to that
work. May we each one pray from our hearts: 'O Lord,
deal with *me*!'

Finally, the end and object of all work to which God
can commit Himself must be His glory. This means that
we get nothing out of it for ourselves. It is a divine principle that the less we get of personal gratification out of
such a work the greater is its true value to God. There is

no room for glory to man in the work of God. True,
there is a deep, precious joy in any service that brings
Him pleasure and that opens the door to His working,
but the ground of that joy is His glory and not man's.
Everything is 'to the praise of the glory of his grace'
(1. 6, 12, 14).

It is when these questions are truly settled between us
and God that God will commit Himself—and indeed I
believe He will allow us to say that then He *has* to do so.
Experience in China has taught us this, that if there is
ground for doubt whether our work is of God, then sure
enough we find God is reluctant to answer prayer in relation to it. But when it is wholly of Him, He will commit
Himself in wonderful ways. Then it is that, in utter obedience to Him, you can use His name, and all Hell will
have to recognise your authority to do so. When God
commits Himself to a thing, then He comes out in power
to prove that He is in it and is Himself its Author.


## THE GOD OF ELIJAH

Let me give you in closing an experience of my own.
A few years after the beginning of our work we entered
upon a period of severe testing. They were days of dis-
appointment and near-despair. We had come in for a
great deal of criticism and discredit on account of the
stand we were taking, resulting in coolness and estrange-
ment, even on the part of the Lord's true people. We had
honestly faced and examined the charges made against us,
for it is essential always to take criticism seriously and
examine it, and not to pass it off with 'Oh! he's just
*criticising* me!' Yet we had reason to believe that the Lord
was with us, for, as a particularly difficult year drew to its
close, we were able to reckon that within that period He

had given us several hundreds of real conversions. Then, at the year's end, it seemed that a climax was reached.

Annually for several years it had been our custom at the New Year public holiday to hold a convention in the city for believers of different connections from throughout the province. This year the sponsors of the convention asked me not to attend. The request came as a shock to us. It was, I now realise, an attempt by the Evil One to draw me and my brethren off our ground of rest in Christ. The question was, how would we react?

The New Year holiday is a long one, lasting fully fifteen days, and besides being a suitable period for a convention, it is also the best time for Gospel preaching. After seeking the Lord's will we became clear that He would have us use it for the latter purpose, so I planned to take with me five brothers for a fifteen-day preaching visit to an island off the South China coast. At the last moment another young brother whom I shall call 'brother Wu' joined the party. He was only sixteen years of age and had been expelled from school, but he had just lately been born again and there was a marked change in his life. Moreover he was very eager to come, so after some hesitation I agreed to take him. This made us seven in all.

The island was a fairly large one with a big main village of 'six thousand stoves'. An old school-mate of mine was there as headmaster of the village school, and I wrote to him in advance asking for a room in which we might lodge during our stay from January 1st to 15th. When however we arrived, late and in darkness, and when he discovered we had come for Gospel preaching, he refused us accommodation. So we sought through the village for somewhere to lodge, until eventually a Chinese herbalist had pity on us and took us in, making us quite comfortable on planks and straw in his attic.

It was not long before the herbalist became our first convert. But though we laboured systematically and hard, and though we found the people of the village most courteous, we had very little fruit from the island, and we began to wonder why this was.

On January 9th we were outside preaching. Brother Wu with some others was in one part of the village and suddenly asked publicly: 'Why will none of you believe?' Someone in the crowd replied at once: 'We have a god— *one* god—Ta-wang,* and he has never failed us. He is an effective god.' 'How do you know that you can trust him?' asked Wu. 'We have held his festival procession every January for 286 years. The chosen day is revealed by divination beforehand, and every year without fail his Day is a perfect one without rain or cloud,' was the reply. 'When is the procession this year?' 'It is fixed for January 11th at eight in the morning.' 'Then,' said brother Wu impetuously, 'I promise you that it will certainly rain on the 11th.' At once there was an outburst of cries from the crowd: 'That is enough! We don't want to hear any more preaching. If there is rain on the 11th, then your God is God!'

I was elsewhere in the village when this occurred. As soon as I heard of it I saw that it was most serious. The news had spread like wildfire, and before long over twenty thousand people would know about it. What were we to do? We stopped our preaching at once, and gave ourselves to prayer. We asked the Lord to forgive us if we had overstepped ourselves. I tell you, we were in deadly earnest. What had we done? Had we made a terrible mistake, or dare we ask God for a miracle?

The more you want an answer to prayer from God, the

* Pronounced with a long *a* as in 'car' and with the final *ng* very lightly sounded. The name means 'Great King'.—ED.

more you desire to be clear with Him. There must be no
doubt about fellowship—no shadow between. If your
faith were in coincidence you could afford to have a con-
troversy with Him, but not otherwise. We did not mind
being thrown out if we had done something wrong. After
all, you can't drag God into a thing against His will! But,
we reflected, this would mean an end to the Gospel testimony in the island, and Ta-wang would reign supreme for
ever. What should we do? Should we leave now?

Up to this point we had feared to pray for rain. Then,
like a flash, there came the word to me: 'Where is the God
of Elijah?' It came with such clarity and power that I
knew it was from God. Confidently I announced to the
brothers: 'I have the answer. The Lord will send rain on
the 11th.' Together we thanked Him, and then, full of
praise, we went out—all seven of us—and told everyone.
We could accept the devil's challenge in the name of the
Lord, and we would broadcast our acceptance.

That evening the herbalist made two very pointed ob-
servations. Undoubtedly, he said, Ta-wang *was* an effective god. The devil was with that image. Their faith in
him was not groundless. Alternatively, if you preferred a
rationalistic explanation, here was a whole village of
fishermen. For two or three months on end the men were
at sea, and on the 15th they would be out again. They, of
all people, should know by long experience when it would
not rain for two or three days ahead.

This disturbed us. As we went to our evening prayer,
we all began once more to pray for rain—*now*! Then it
was that there came to us a stern rebuke from the Lord:
'Where is the God of Elijah?' Were we going to fight our
way through this battle, or were we going to rest in the
finished victory of Christ? What had Elisha done when
he spoke those words? He had laid claim in his own per-

sonal experience to the very miracle that his lord Elijah,
now in the glory, had himself performed. In New Testament terms, he had taken his stand by faith on the ground
of a finished work.

We confessed our sins again. 'Lord,' we said, 'we don't
need rain until the 11th morning.' We went to bed, and
next morning (the 10th) we set off for a neighbouring
island for a day's preaching. The Lord was very gracious,
and that day three families turned to Him, confessing Him
publicly and burning their idols. We returned late, tired
out but rejoicing. We could afford to sleep late tomorrow.

I was awakened by the direct rays of the sun through
the single window of our attic. 'This isn't rain!' I said. It
was already past seven o'clock. I got up, knelt down and
prayed. 'Lord,' I said, 'please send the rain!' But once
again, ringing in my ears came the word: 'Where is the
God of Elijah?' Humbled, I walked downstairs before
God in silence. We sat down to breakfast—eight of us
together, including our host—all very quiet. There was
no cloud in the sky, but we knew God was committed.
As we bowed to say grace before the food I said, 'I think
the time is up. Rain must come now. We can bring it to
the Lord's remembrance.' Quietly we did so, and this
time the answer came with no hint whatever of rebuke
in it.

'*Where is the God of Elijah?*' Even before our Amen we
heard a few drops on the tiles. There was a steady shower
as we ate our rice and were served with a second bowl.
'Let us give thanks again,' I said, and now we asked God
for heavier rain. As we began on that second bowl of rice
the rain was coming down in buckets-full. By the time
we had finished, the street outside was already deep in
water and the three steps at the door of the house were
covered.

Soon we heard what had happened in the village. Already, at the first drop of rain, a few of the younger generation had begun to say openly: 'There is God; there is no more Ta-wang! He is kept in by the rain.' But he wasn't. They carried him out on a sedan chair. Surely he would stop the shower! Then came the downpour. After only some ten or twelve yards, three of the coolies stumbled and fell. Down went the chair and Ta-wang with it, fracturing his jaw and his left arm. Still determined, they carried out emergency repairs and put him back in the chair. Somehow, slipping and stumbling, they dragged or carried him half-way round the village. Then the floods defeated them. Some of the village elders, old men of 60 to 80 years, bareheaded and without umbrellas as their faith in Ta-wang's weather required, had fallen and were in serious difficulties. The procession was stopped and the idol taken into a house. Divination was made. 'Today was the wrong day,' came the answer. 'The festival is to be on the 14th with the procession at six in the evening.'

Immediately we heard this there came the assurance in our hearts: 'God will send rain on the 14th.' We went to prayer: 'Lord, send rain on the 14th at 6.0 p.m. and give us four good days until then.' That afternoon the sky cleared, and now we had a good hearing for the Gospel. The Lord gave us over thirty converts—real ones—in the village and in the island during those three short days. The 14th broke, another perfect day, and we had good meetings. As the evening approached we met, and again, at the appointed hour, we quietly brought the matter to the Lord's remembrance. Not a minute late, His answer came with torrential rain and floods as before.

The next day our time was up and we had to leave. We have not been back. Other workers asked for those islands and we never question anyone's claim to a field. But for us the essential point was that Satan's power in that idol had been broken, and that is an eternal thing. Ta-wang was no more 'an effective god'. The salvation of souls would follow, but was in itself secondary to this vital and unchanging fact.

The impression on us all was a lasting one. God had committed Himself. We had tasted the authority of the name that is above every name—the name that has power in heaven and earth and hell. In those few days we had known what it is to be, as we say, 'in the very centre of the will of God'. Those words were no longer something vague or visionary to us. They described an experience we had ourselves been through. Together we had been granted a brief glimpse of 'the mystery of his will' (1. 9; 3. 10). We would go softly all our days. Years later I met 'brother Wu'. I had lost touch with him, and in the interval he had become a pilot in the Airways. When I asked him whether he still followed the Lord, 'Mr Nee!' he said, 'do you mean to say that after all we went through I could ever forsake Him?'

Do you see what it means to 'stand'? We do not try to gain ground; we merely stand on the ground which the Lord Jesus has gained for us, and resolutely refuse to be moved from it. When our eyes are really opened to see Christ as our victorious Lord, then our praise flows forth freely and without restraint. Singing with melody in our hearts to the Lord, we give thanks for all things in His name (5. 19–20). Praise that is the outcome of effort has a laboured and discordant note, but praise that wells up spontaneously from hearts at rest in Him has always a pure, sweet tone.

The Christian life consists of sitting with Christ, walking by Him and standing in Him. We begin our spiritual life by resting in the finished work of the Lord Jesus. That rest is the source of our strength for a consistent and unfaltering walk in the world. And at the end of a gruelling warfare with the hosts of darkness we are found standing with Him at last in triumphant possession of the field.

'Unto him . . . be the glory . . . for ever.'